To

ELY and DOROTHY GORDON

who, in youth, left homes and families and all that was
familiar to them in the Crimea, and came to Canada –
the first of their many gifts to their children

T0339327

SOCIAL SCIENCE AND MODERN MAN

The main theme of these lectures is man's struggle to understand himself as a social being. The author argues that the chief inspiration for this effort, insofar as it has been successful, has been the rationalist philosophy of physical science, and that constructive social science has been based on this philosophy rather than upon theology and ethical philosophy. He goes on to discuss the major problems confronting man in his attempts to come to grips with the modern social world – problems of social and political organization, of equality and aspiration, of intellect and reason – and ends with a plea for liberalism and rationalism as the political and intellectual foundations of freedom and progress. This fascinating and thought-provoking apology for liberalism and the social scientist will be valuable reading for anyone interested in problems facing them both today.

SCOTT GORDON received his A. M. from Columbia University in 1947 and his PH.D. from McGill University in 1964. He taught at Carleton University in Ottawa from 1948 to 1966, and was a visiting professor at the University of Chicago (1956–57) and Purdue University (1967–68). He is at present Professor of Economics and Associate Member of the Department of History and Philosophy of Science at Indiana University. He has written many journal articles, has contributed chapters to several books, and is the author of *The Economists Versus the Bank of Canada.*

SCOTT GORDON

Social Science & Modern Man

ALAN B. PLAUNT MEMORIAL LECTURES
CARLETON UNIVERSITY
1969

PUBLISHED BY UNIVERSITY OF TORONTO PRESS
IN CO-OPERATION WITH CARLETON UNIVERSITY

© University of Toronto Press 1970
Reprinted in paperback 2017
University of Toronto Press
Toronto and Buffalo
ISBN 978-0-8020-1675-1 (cloth)
ISBN 978-1-4875-9908-9 (paper)

Contents

Contents

Preface

When President Dunton asked me, after I had accepted his invitation to be Carleton University's Plaunt lecturer for 1969, what the title of my lectures would be, I cudgelled my brains for a while and then said 'Social Science and Modern Man.' Now, a title as broad as this usually means that the speaker doesn't know for sure what he is going to talk about and is keeping all the options open.

The lectures are now in cold print and I should be able to say more definitely what they are about, but the fact is that I am still not certain – so I have decided to keep the original title.

In general, what I want to discuss is one of the most important aspects of man's fairly recent intellectual history – the rise of social science. Alexander Pope, in the eighteenth century, announced that 'the proper study of mankind is man.' Well, proper or not, economists and sociologists have been very busy at it during the past two centuries, and social science is, today, one of the great facts of modern civilization. Needless to say, a lot of other areas of study have also undergone a great development as well but it is social science I want to focus on both as an historical phenomenon and, in particular, its relation to the rather special problems which emerge in societies like Canada, which are economically and technically highly advanced and which have achieved a high degree of individual freedom and political democracy.

I want first to deal with these things in a very general way, and to discuss the broad problems which man seems to encounter in a highly developed society. In the second part I want to focus more concretely on social policy – that is, our efforts to act as collective beings – and to consider how we may develop a philosophy of social policy that is adequate to the modern world.

S.G.

SOCIAL SCIENCE AND MODERN MAN

ONE

Children of the Age of Reason

I would like to begin by trying to make clear what I have in mind when I speak of "social science," and in order to do so I will have to recall some of the general intellectual history of western man.

In one way of looking at it, the study of social phenomena is the oldest and most continuous of man's intellectual pursuits. The ancient books of religion, like the Old Testament, may be regarded as dealing with man's relation to God, but much more acutely they deal with man's relation to his fellows, i.e. with *social* relations. A large part of the classical writings of the Golden Age of Greek civilization deal with social and political questions. Much of the immense theological literature of medieval Europe is focused on the problems raised by man's social relations rather than the problems of his soul.

If we were to regard all of this literature as early social science, as some historians do, we would not be able to distinguish between the study of man as undertaken by the poet or the novelist or by the theologian and philosopher, and the study undertaken by the economist, the sociologist, and the statistician. It is true that we all labour in the same vineyard in the sense that we all endeavour to understand the human condition and we all hope to assist man to become a more civilized being. So much can be granted. But the nature of modern social science and the significance of its development, cannot be appreciated if we view it simply as an extension of the ancient study of man which has merely given itself some pretentious new names and titles.

My first point, therefore, is that what we today call 'social science' is a new intellectual phenomenon in the history of man, not much more than two centuries old. A great deal of social science, when it was in its infancy in the eighteenth century, was classified under the headings of 'moral philosophy' and 'theology,' but its true intellectual lineage goes back not to these subjects, but to the physical sciences. When Kepler and Newton and Descartes laid the foundations for modern physical science, they unwittingly laid the foundations for social science as well. When they detached the study of physical phenomena from theology, and made physics and chemistry possible, they also enabled us to detach the study of social phenomena from theology, and made economics and sociology possible as well.

This separation of science from theology was a long time coming about; and it was not *recognized* to be an accomplished fact until late in the nineteenth century. One of the striking things that occurs to a reader of the older literature is the strong and almost universal view one finds there that God was regarded as an *immediate presence* in the world. Logically, this should have led people to practise continuous worship and to devote their lives to supplication, in fear of divine power. But in western Europe the view took hold, in some corners, that the Christian God was disciplined and orderly – not the capricious or moody or peevish divinity of the Greek Pantheon or of Israel's Jehovah – and this led to the study of *nature* as a manifestation of His divine discipline. For a time, the theistic and scientific attitudes were fused. To put questions to nature by means of careful observation and experiment was regarded as equivalent to conversing with God. On this basis, scientific knowledge grew and grew, rapidly and deeply. By the time it was realized that it was not God who was answering the questions of these investigators, it was too late to go back. Science existed, and it had its own credentials of legitimacy, independent of theology. Rationalism and empiricism were firmly established as the basic modes of knowledge. In the eighteenth century, the study of social phenomena began to place itself upon the same foundations.

The scientific approach is such a large part of modern life that it is difficult to believe that man's intellectual attitude was ever different. I want to take a moment to emphasize this point. To give some idea of how the educated mind worked even as recently as the end of the seventeenth century, I include an account of the medical treatment of King Charles ɪɪ upon his final illness in 1685. The account is based on the records of a Dr. Scarburgh, one of the King's physicians, and is contained in H. W. Haggard, *Devils, Drugs and Doctors*:

At eight o'clock on Monday morning of February 2, 1685, King Charles was being shaved in his bedroom. With a sudden cry he fell backward and had a violent convulsion. He became unconscious, rallied once or twice, and after a few days died. Seventeenth-century autopsy records are far from complete, but

5

one could hazard a guess that the king suffered from an embolism – that is, a floating blood clot which had plugged up an artery and deprived some portion of his brain of blood – or else his kidneys were diseased. As the first step in treatment the king was bled to the extent of a pint from a vein in his right arm. Next his shoulder was cut into and the incised area 'cupped' to suck out an additional eight ounces of blood. After this homicidal onslaught, the drugging began. An emetic and purgative were administered, and soon after a second purgative. This was followed by an enema containing antimony, sacred bitters, rock salt, mallow leaves, violets, beet roots, camomile flowers, fennel seed, linseed, cinnamon cardamon seed, saphron, cochineal, and aloes. The enema was repeated in two hours and a purgative given. The king's head was shaved and a blister raised in his scalp. A sneezing powder of hellebore root was administered, and also a powder of cowslip flowers 'to strengthen his brain.' The cathartics were repeated at frequent intervals and interspersed with a soothing drink composed of barley water, licorice and sweet almond. Likewise white wine, absinthe and anise were given, as also were extracts of thistle leaves, mint, rue, and angelica. For external treatment a plaster of Burgundy pitch and pigeon dung were applied to the king's feet. The bleeding and purging continued, and to the medicaments were added melon seeds, manna, slippery elm, black cherry water, an extract of flowers of lime, lily-of-the-valley, peony, lavender, and dissolved pearls. Later came gentian root, nutmeg, quinine, and cloves. The king's condition did not improve, indeed it grew worse, and in the emergency forty drops of extract of human skull were administered to allay convulsions. A rallying dose of Raleigh's antidote was forced down the King's throat; this antidote contained an enormous number of herbs and animal extracts. Finally bezoar stone was given. Then, says Scarburgh: 'Alas! after an ill-fated night his serene majesty's strength seemed exhausted to such a degree that the whole assembly of physicians lost all hope and became despondent: still so as not to appear to fail in doing their duty in any detail, they brought into play the most active cordial.' As a sort of grand summary to this pharmaceutical debauch, a mixture of Raleigh's antidote, pearl julep, and ammonia was forced down the throat of the dying king.

Now what are we to make of this? We cannot dismiss the physicians of Charles II as fools. On the contrary, they represented the best medical knowledge of the time, and they were not dealing with abstract metaphysics but with very practical matters. Their 'knowledge,' however, if we can give it that name, seems to have been nothing more than a collection of ancient nostrums. These physicians lacked a sound foundation for their practice because the spirit of scientific study of the human body had not yet been established. If one considers how far removed modern medicine is from the account I have just read, one can get at least a slight idea of the intellectual change that has taken place in the last three centuries.

There is another aspect of this intellectual change that I want to bring to your attention, one that is more difficult to explain briefly, but is very important for what I am trying to get at.

In order to understand the mind of the pre-scientific era, one must understand the general belief in the existence of occult powers in the world. A book that is especially revealing for this purpose is Aldous Huxley's *The Devils of Loudun*. It is an account of a celebrated case of 'demonic possession' which took place in the French town of Loudun, near Tours, in the early seventeenth century. The nuns of the town's Carmelite convent suddenly began to act rather strangely, and a local priest, one Urbain Grandier, was accused of having entered into a pact with the devil in order to torment them. After interrogation and torture, the unfortunate Grandier was eventually burnt alive for witchcraft.

The important part of this dark story is the care with which the charge was investigated by the ecclesiastical authorities. The Church demanded hard evidence, and it got it. The nuns 'spoke in tongues'; 'stigmata' appeared on their bodies; they performed feats of incredible strength and endurance while 'possessed.' In fact, we don't require as much proof today in modern courts of law; we hang people on less evidence than that on which Grandier was burnt. The difference between our century and the seventeenth is not a matter of evidence and proof but the simple fact that there is no place for occult powers in our mental image of the world. Science has exorcised the devil by leaving no room for him in its model of reality. It is not a matter of one age being illogical and another logical. It is a matter of fundamental belief – one's basic image of the constitution of nature.

How difficult it is for us to grasp the mind of an age that believed in occult powers is indicated by the effort, a few years ago, to turn Huxley's book into a stage play in New York. It was a failure as a play despite the acting talents of Jason Robards and Anne Bancroft because the playwright and director simply could not bring themselves to believe that anybody had *ever* believed in witchcraft. In an effort to make the events at Loudun three hundred years ago intelligible to a twentieth-century mind they interpreted Huxley's book in modern terms. The demonic frenzies of the Carmelite nuns became a simple case of sexual repression among ladies of enforced celibacy. The investigative tenacity of the church inquisitor became a simple matter of ambition to get on in the world and be promoted in the hierarchy by doing a thorough job of his assignment. As a result the play conveyed no understanding of the seventeenth century mind at all.

The theme of the conflict between medieval theology and the rational empiricism of science was also explored in *Lamp at Midnight*, a Broadway play on Galileo's celebrated struggle with the Church. It had the great advantage of Tyrone Guthrie as director, but it too only succeeded in proving how hard it is for the modern mind to grasp the system of thought which was held almost universally by intelligent and educated men in the pre-scientific age.

Why am I wandering around in the dark mental processes of the seventeenth century like this? Because I want to emphasize that the intellectual attitudes we take for granted in modern civilized societies are recent in the history of man. A momentous change has taken place in our mental life in the past few centuries. Intellectually, we are not the descendants of the Golden Age of Athens, or of the Judaeo-Christian tradition in theology. We are the children of the Age of Science, and the Age of Reason.

But we are not quite sure what that means. The great historian W. E. H. Lecky wrote a large book, *The Rise and Influence of Rationalism in Europe*. When we come to the end of its eight hundred pages we are sure that something tremendous happened, but what it is and how it occurred remains a mystery. All that Lecky can say, when we come down to it, is that there was a change in man's 'predisposition to believe.' That is to say, we do not believe in occult powers today because we are not predisposed to accept such arguments even if they are supported by evidence. The great eighteenth-century philosopher, David Hume, expressed the modern temper exactly in his famous essay on miracles. Should we believe in miracles, he asked, even when presented with evidence? Suppose that all the historians and chroniclers agreed that Queen Elizabeth had returned from the dead. What should we believe? This was Hume's advice:

I should not doubt her pretended death, and of those other public circumstances that followed it: I should simply assert it to have been pretended, and that it neither was nor possibly could be real ... I would ... reply, that the knavery and folly of men are such common phenomena, that I should rather believe the most extraordinary events to arise from their concurrence, than admit of so signal a violation of the laws of nature.

Here is the heart of the matter – there are *laws of nature* which cannot be violated by man or devil or God.

Once the physical sciences had succeeded in establishing this conception of the physical world, it was possible to extend it to the world of human behaviour and social phenomena. There are laws of human nature and social nature too, and so there can be social science, just as there is physical science.

The victory of the scientific attitude has not, of course, been complete. There still exist mystery sects like the Rosicrucians, and astrology still enjoys a considerable body of devotees. Even in practical matters like medicine, we have Christian

Scientists, and Queen Elizabeth II has recently appointed a homeopath to the staff of physicians to the Royal household. Even among the intelligent and the sophisticated, there are those who believe they can attain direct cosmic revelation via Zen Buddhism, or hallucinogenic drugs, or other "mind-expanding" experiences. There are still people who believe literally in the existence of occult powers. I read in the Toronto *Globe and Mail* of 25 January 1969 (not 1669) that three Roman Catholic priests were called to investigate certain strange happenings in a house in Acton Vale, Quebec. They reported, it is quoted: 'In our view, it is the case of a diabolical phenomenon, a rare phenomenon, but possible with divine permission ... The Devil, if God allows it, can manifest himself tangibly ... (and) the gravity of a diabolical infestation depends on the latitude God has given the Spirit of Evil to try His servants.' In Switzerland, a man and woman belonging to a sect described as the International Community for the Furtherance of Peace were jailed recently for beating a young girl to death in an effort to drive the devil out of her body.

I think it is fair to say though that, so far as physical phenomena are concerned, the modes of thought of rationalist science are now deeply established. Even the members of the Flat Earth Society consider it necessary to offer alternative mechanical models of the universe to explain their belief that Apollo VIII did not go round the moon and back. But by comparison with physical science, the rationalist roots of social science are still shallow. Large numbers of people view social phenomena as manifestations of forces which are really the political equivalent of demonic powers. The conspiratorial theory of politics enjoys a certain substantial vogue. A few

11

years ago, Arthur Miller wrote a play, *The Crucible*, about the New England witchcraft craze of the seventeenth century; it was a much more successful work of art than the effort to dramatize Huxley's *Devils of Loudun* or Galileo's struggles with the Church in *Lamp at Midnight* because it had an authentic modern referent: the revival of medievalism that was inherent in the political hysteria of McCarthyism in the United States in the 1950s. One would like to think that this is a cast of mind confined to the ignorant and the gullible, but alas, one finds otherwise intelligent and sceptical people embracing political philosophies which they regard as disclosing in one flash of light the whole demonology of the social and economic world, in terms of categories such as the 'establishment' or 'imperialism' or the 'military-industrial complex' or sometimes with grand comprehensiveness, the 'system.' Not without evidence, of course; evidence almost as good as that which the priests of Acton Vale saw with their very eyes. Nor can we assume with assurance that pre-rationalist or anti-rationalist modes of social thought will always remain a minority comprehension in a modern nation. There is, after all, the experience of German Naziism to give one pause.

Social phenomena are complex and no more self-evident than physical phenomena. To the naïve observer, the flies that gather on the window pane are obviously trying to get *out*; and the moon is more valuable to man than the sun because it shines at night when the light is really needed. The social scientist tries to pierce the obvious, to discover the *laws* of social phenomena, but there are many who hold the view that to 'unmask' the conspirators and the manipulators of the world is all that needs be done.

I cannot go much further with this, because of the laws delimiting my time (and space), but perhaps I have succeeded in indicating the drift of my argument. Social science, to my mind, is an outgrowth of the rationalist age, which was initiated and established by physical science. The rationalistic study of man has, however, not driven its roots as deep into the civilized intellect as has the scientific study of physical phenomena. It could easily be uprooted in a prolonged political hurricane.

I have been describing social science so far in the singular, but it is, of course, a plural subject with a number of branches represented by different departments in a typical modern university. You will perhaps not be surprised if I claim that the virtues and merits I see in social science generally are particularly notable in my own field of economics. Economics is not only a rationalist study of man, but it is the study of man *as a rational being*. To the economist, the buying and selling that goes on in markets, and the producing and consuming that goes on behind and before them, are conceived of as manifestations of man's capacity for the rational organization of his daily life. What makes sense to an economist is the view that man is a maximizing creature, trying to achieve some definite objective as fully as he can in a world which presents him with various constraints and limitations. Some important consequences flow from this, and these I would like to discuss briefly.

First, since we cannot have everything we want, we must make choices. The constraints and limitations imposed by the external world force man to be rational, that is to say, to make logically effective choices. Some economists today even define the content of economic theory as 'the logic of rational choice.'

It isn't a bad definition; it catches the spirit of a lot of the work that economists do. It is deeply imbedded into the structure of economic theory that this process of rational choice will produce variety. We will not find a rational man or a rational society devoting itself exclusively to one thing. The society that dedicates itself without reserve to power, or prestige, or glory, is as irrational as the man who dedicates himself to whisky. Whenever someone says that something is immeasurably important, or infinitely valuable, or priceless, one can see an economist's hackles rise. Economics is the enemy of absolutes, and that applies to political and social aims as well as to material ones.

Secondly, it is inherent in the structure of economic theory that only individuals can make value judgments. A society or a nation is not a sentient organism able to enjoy and appreciate or make aesthetic and moral determinations; only men and women can do that. The significance of this individualistic postulate is that it quickly leads one to the corollary that all men should be treated equally as valuing beings. Consequently, there are strong democratic and egalitarian elements inherent in the basic logic of economics. With very few exceptions, economists have been committed democrats since Adam Smith's time.

Finally, I wish to point out that economics contains a strong cosmopolitan element. We talk about the *national* income and the *national* welfare, and we advise on policies that are in the best interests of our own nation state. But the nation is really a pragmatic rather than a fundamental unit in economic theory. From its earliest days in the late eighteenth century, scientific economics has had an international orientation, and one of its most notable achievements is the demonstration of the mutuality of the economic interests of individual nations.

In sum then, I see economics (and I think I might be able to say the same for sociology as well) as a study of man which is committed to liberalism, democracy and cosmopolitanism. At the end of the eighteenth century, the English political philosopher, Edmund Burke, moaned that 'the age of chivalry is gone. That of sophisters, economists and calculators, has succeeded and the glory of Europe is extinguished forever.' How wrong he was! The age of chivalry was just beginning, and 'economists and calculators' were destined to play a large role in it. That role is not yet ended.

TWO

Modern Problems

I have perhaps tried your patience enough by dealing in such general terms with social science and intellectual history. I would now like to turn to the specific and focus attention on more concrete issues of contemporary concern. There are, it seems to me, a number of developments which have emerged as problems in economically advanced and politically democratic societies. In an effort to cope with them for the purposes of these lectures, I have attempted to package them under the following labels: (1) the Brave New World Problem; (2) the Affluent Society Problem; (3) the Entrenched Oligarchy Problem; and (4) the Problem of Professionalism. Each of these will be discussed in turn.

THE BRAVE NEW WORLD PROBLEM

A one-armed social scientist would be a terribly maimed creature, for there are hardly any of us who can get very far without saying 'on the other hand.' Having just sung the praises of social science and covered myself and my colleagues with honour as the most rational and humane spirits of the modern age, it is only to be expected that I will now go on to say 'however, on the other hand, ...' There is an obverse to the face of our intellectual heritage that I have been showing you, and it seems to become more important every day that we take note of it.

I have called this 'the Brave New World Problem' because the best presentation of it that I know is in Aldous Huxley's novel of that name written in the early 1930s. Most people seem to remember this novel as a picture of society which is horrifying because motherhood has been made obsolete by science. The inhabitants of Huxley's world (it is not certain that we should call them 'people') are of two sexes and possess the requisite equipment and capacity for sexual enjoyment, but they do not do so for the purpose of human reproduction at all, not even incidentally, or indeed, even accidentally. The production of life in this way is regarded as obscene, and has been outlawed. Science has developed much neater, and more efficient, methods of providing the labour and specialized skills required by an industrial society. The required humanoid organisms are produced in test tubes under controlled laboratory conditions where nothing is left to chance. It is a eugenist's dream – and a humanist's nightmare.

If we look a bit closer at Huxley's 'Brave New World,' however, we find that what makes it repulsive is not the success of the biochemist in synthesizing the human reproductive process. This aspect is not really even very shocking when we come down to it. After all, the modern educational system is not essentially different from Huxley's test-tubes. We get the raw material out of a womb, but we then convert it into 'human capital' by running it through a mill which grinds, and shapes, and stamps it out into a well-trained engineer, or a computer programmer, or a literary critic, or an economist. We don't even have to contend against parental love in carrying out this process – the modern parent is anxious to shove the little ingot of his adoration into the maw of this machine.

No, what is unsatisfactory in the 'Brave New World,' when one comes down to it, is that the dream of social science has come true to it. Everyone is well fed, well clothed, well housed. There is a great deal of leisure, and many opportunities for enjoyment. There is even provision for variety in tastes – some girls are more 'pneumatic' than others. Everybody is satisfied and happy. Now what can be wrong with that? It is a utilitarian heaven; isn't that what we have been striving for all along?

Nevertheless 'Brave New World' is horrible, as Huxley meant it to be. What is essentially repellent about it is its *flatness*. There is no striving, no yearning, no dreaming or creating. All the tally-ho is organized so that there should be no disappointment, no misadventure, and no pain. Tennyson had his hero Ulysses sigh, 'must we forever climb the climbing wave?' as if he found it a burden, but the plain fact is he wanted to climb, indeed he was compelled to by his human nature. Man is a romantic being. He seeks adventure and danger, fame and glory. He is Don Quixote de la Mancha, and if there were no giants or dragons in the world, he would create some, so that he might fight them.

This is one of the oldest and most persistent themes in our literature. If you read the English poets and novelists of the early nineteenth century you will find that they loathed the world of industrial capitalism and material progress that was coming into being, and they were contemptuous of the philosophy of utilitarianism on which the new social science was founded. Carlyle called it the 'pig philosophy,' but he was only a little more violent in expressing views that were shared by Coleridge, Wordsworth, Tennyson, Dickens, Ruskin and the rest of the English romantics.

In essentials, the romantics were wrong. Economic and material progress is not the enemy of civilization and higher humanism. It would be truer to regard it as a pre-condition. Poverty is not an aesthetic or a moral virtue. Suffering and starvation do not make men wiser and more humane. Fortunately for us today, the great nineteenth-century contention between the utilitarians and the romantics was won by the utilitarians. The romantics may have dominated the world of literature and music and philosophy, but the utilitarians dominated the economy, and, to a somewhat lesser extent, the state.

Nevertheless, the nineteenth-century romantics had their fingers on something of importance, and we are now being forced to recognize their insight into the human condition. The Brave New World Problem, as I have called it, is that we have no reason to believe that man will be satisfied with a state of economic plenty and security. To the adventurous spirit, these are merely bourgeois virtues. Man needs challenges, and enemies.

I sometimes think how simple was the world of my youth compared to that of today. We had two great enemies – the depression and the Germans – big enough, and evil enough, and dangerous enough for anybody's taste. There is no equivalent for them in today's world. Most of our sons and daughters have been brought up in a world of plenty – unlimited food, good clothing and shelter, personal security, education of high quality – and, as a consequence, they feel deprived. The Dutch philosopher Johan Huizinga wrote a book some twenty-five years ago called *Homo Ludens* – man, a game-playing animal – in which he pointed out the significance of play in the culture of man. Today we are very much in need of some good games which would provide excitement and the thrill of contest, but not undermine economic progress, political democracy, or the development of man into a more sensitive and civilized creature. The physicists have made it pretty dangerous for us to play War anymore, and besides that, a lot of us are getting too civilized to enjoy it.

THE AFFLUENT SOCIETY PROBLEM

Under this heading I want to consider a social problem to which John K. Galbraith's book, *The Affluent Society*, brought widespread public attention some ten years ago. It is a very peculiar problem because it almost seems to reverse the general and obvious rule that a wealthy society can provide more material benefits for its citizens than a poor one can. A society that is progressing economically and steadily increasing its general command of economic resources may in fact become *less* capable of serving a certain range of human needs even though, in principle, it is necessary only that the requisite amount of economic resources be devoted to them.

As a society develops economically, and especially as it becomes more urbanized, its need for what economists call 'collective goods' rises. By 'collective goods' we mean goods and services which cannot be provided individually to consumers in response to their individual preferences and needs. A standardized good has to be provided generally for all members of a given community. It is possible for me to exercise my individual taste for food or clothing – I simply go to the shops and buy what suits my own peculiar wants, and every other member of the community can do the same. It is easy for an economy (of any type) to meet the diversity of such needs. But I cannot exercise, in the same way, my preference for something like street cleanliness. I could sweep the street outside my own home, but that is not really what I want; I want the streets of my community *generally* to be clean. In brief, there is no private property in street cleanliness; all members of the community enjoy its benefits collectively.

There are, of course, many goods which are individually consumed, like shirts and socks and steak, but there are also many that are inherently collective, including a large proportion of civic and other governmental services, and some publicly supported goods and services such as the educational system and various cultural and recreational facilities.

The main problem with such collective goods is that it is difficult to manage them and to finance them. The same person who would not drop a cigarette butt in his own driveway, will cheerfully empty the ashtray of his car in the public roadway. The same person who would regard it as barbarous not to send his children to school will wiggle like an eel to avoid the taxes which must be levied to pay for such collective goods as schools. (The city of Youngstown, Ohio had to close its public school system for the last month of 1968 because it did not have the money to pay its expenses. This occurred not in Appalachia or in Mississippi, but in a modern and prosperous industrial city which enjoys the full fruits of the past decade of rapid economic growth. The people of Youngstown simply refused to vote the taxes necessary to pay for their schools!)

22

There is another aspect of this problem which will, I think, greatly exacerbate the difficulty of providing an adequate level of public services and other collective goods. It arises from the fact that a large proportion of these goods and services are 'labour intensive,' as economists say, and it is not possible to increase by much the productivity of labour in such lines of activity. This gives rise to what has been called 'Baumol's disease' after William J. Baumol of Princeton who used the idea a few years ago to explain why the performing arts are experiencing greater and greater financial difficulty as the society they serve becomes wealthier and wealthier.

Let me try to explain this phenomenon by reference to the problem of education where, I believe, it will have some of its most acute impact in the next few years.

As a society progresses economically, its output per man rises. So, the wages of automobile workers, and steelworkers, and textile workers, and others, go up. But this means that the salaries of teachers and professors must go up too, if for no other reason than to draw the requisite manpower into the education industry. But if we maintain the same ratio of teachers to students as before, the cost of providing the education *per student* will rise, and it will keep on rising as long as economic progress continues, even without any improvement in the quality of the educational services provided. Automobiles and shirts may not rise in price because technical improvements mean an increase of car and shirt output per man, but if we do not increase the number of students 'processed' per teacher, and, in my opinion, we cannot do so without reducing the quality of education, particularly at elementary school levels, then we have to be prepared to face the necessity of providing *more money per student every year* just to maintain the existing quality of education.

This problem is not peculiar to education. It will be faced by all parts of the economy that are labour-intensive, from barber shops to ballet companies. Unfortunately, since a large part of the public services financed by taxation are labour-intensive, we may well discover that they are squeezed between the increasing costs due to 'Baumol's disease' on the one hand, and the reluctance of people to tax themselves for the provision of collective goods and services on the other.

This problem is already with us – 'private affluence and public squalor' it has been called. The public sector of our society becomes more and more squalid as the private sector becomes more and more affluent. The picture of community life, and particularly urban life, that this trend generates is not attractive. I have the impression that this problem is, so far, more acute in the United States than in Canada, but it is a general problem inherent in the characteristics of economic progress itself. This problem of public finance is not so serious for those levels of government which receive a large proportion of their revenues from progressively scheduled income taxes, for these will automatically yield more revenues as economic growth takes place. It will be the junior governments, and especially the cities, that will really feel the pinch, but even at the federal level, the willingness of the public to levy increased taxes upon themselves is a pre-condition of social progress in a modern world. Any economically advanced society that fails to develop the higher level of community consciousness necessary to support a marked improvement in the finance and administration of public services and other collective goods will be an uncivilized place – dirty, ugly, ignorant, and unsafe – despite, indeed partly *because* of, its technical and economic progress.

Perhaps I should have called this 'the King Midas Problem?'

THE ENTRENCHED OLIGARCHY PROBLEM

I would now like to go on to discuss, necessarily with brevity, the problem of maintaining and promoting a high degree of social mobility in our society.

For the past two centuries or so, man has been living in exceedingly fluid societies. Revolutions have taken place all over the world – economic revolutions and political revolutions – and today there is hardly a corner that has not experienced the displacement of old hardened institutions and the establishment of new economic systems, new social practices, and new political authorities.

In Canada, and in the countries that have been of principal importance in Canadian social and economic development, that is, Great Britain and the United States, the revolutionary developments which created the mobility and fluidity I am talking about were almost exclusively economic in origin. It is true, the British went so far as to cut off a foolish monarch's head in the seventeenth century, but nothing really changed very much so far as the mass of the people were concerned. The United States was born in a revolution which had immense political and international consequences, but, again, I don't think it can be said that the structure and dynamics of American society were much affected by it. The Daughters of the American Revolution were not so silly as they seemed a few years ago when, despite their name, they passed a declaration condemning all revolutions. As far as Canada's only effort in that direction was concerned, we didn't even get as far as to knock off a bishop's mitre.

The extraordinary social fluidity of these countries has been due to their industrial revolutions, not their political ones. In England, before the late eighteenth century, there existed a fusion of economic and political power that was almost complete. Its basis was *land*. Ownership of land conferred wealth and economic power and it determined social status and political authority as well. What the industrial revolution did was to permit the growth of economic wealth on a large scale outside the orbit of landed power, and this produced in the society a degree of mobility hitherto unknown or even dreamed of. North America was an even more fluid society than Britain. Except in the American South and possibly in French Canada, social and economic power never did become firmly connected with land, and, anyway, since land was not limited in supply there could be no monopoly of it of the sort necessary to social exclusiveness.

As a result of the economic growth which has characterized the past century, our societies have continued to be quite fluid. Not perfectly so of course. Indeed far from it. We have never been even within telescopic distance of a society of complete equality of opportunity, but we are now a lot closer to it than at any previous time in human history.

In the late nineteenth century, many Americans became exceedingly worried that their society might be closing and hardening. They saw the development of an entrenched oligarchy of plutocratic businessmen, using the newly developed laws of corporate organization to establish 'trusts,' as they were then called, and to fix themselves forever into economic and political power. Mark Twain, the great iconoclast, wrote about it in his first novel, *The Gilded Age*, in which he not only flayed the shallow mammonism of his society, but sounded the alarm that the men of business had corrupted politics and were seizing political power for themselves. He didn't think much of the intelligence of congressmen and senators and even less of their morals. He wasn't alone in this; the literature and journalism on this theme was a flourishing industry at the time.

The rule of the trusts didn't take place in the United States, partly because they were attacked by law, partly because of the growth of trade unions as independent centres of power, but mainly because the economy continued to expand and to generate innovations in products and in methods of production which kept the established business enterprises off balance and prevented them from consolidating their power. It may be that we can depend on continued economic change to keep advanced industrial societies from developing into hardened oligarchies, but there are times when I am not optimistic about this. It seems to me that certain developments have taken place already, and are continuing, which will have a strong tendency to reduce social mobility in countries such as Canada and the United States. I can't talk about this extensively here, but I would like to sketch the outlines of what I have in mind.

The most important development in social organization during the past half century or so is the growth of bureaucracy. I am not referring only to government when I use this term. The bureaucratic form of organization has become solidly established in modern business and industry, in trade unions, in the professions, in education, and in almost everything else. It is in these bureaucracies that power resides. The political, economic and social functions of our society are becoming increasingly concentrated within a limited number of these bureaucracies, which tend to become, as a result, the dominant established institutions of society, just as the Church and the aristocracy were in earlier times.

Modern bureaucracies may appear to be very different from the medieval Church and aristocracy but they share certain common characteristics in respect of the crucial question of the recruitment of new members to occupy senior positions of authority within their structures. Like the Church, modern bureaucracies recruit into themselves people who appear to be reliable perpetuators of their established practices. Senior bureaucrats invite people who are like themselves to share and to inherit power. Like the ancient aristocrat, the modern bureaucrat is particularly anxious to see to it that his own children are well placed. I am not saying that deputy ministers and general managers hand over their jobs directly to their sons, or that union presidents bequeath the union to theirs. That is not necessary. The same general result is produced if the bureaucrat in one establishment enables his son to get a good start on the hierarchical ladder in another. In our society, it is virtually impossible for the children of a successful man to fall down into the pool of common labour, unless they are determined to do so. The children of the lower classes have to work hard to be successes. The children of the middle and upper classes have to make great efforts to be failures.

The result of this is that the bureaucracies which make up

the established institutions of modern society tend to become dominated by entrenched oligarchies. The children of the poor and the rejected have never had a fair shake in the social crap game; they are going to get an even worse one if we do not make strong efforts to increase the fluidity of society. There is one feature of modern social organization which could be used to exert a great deal of leverage in this direction. All the bureaucracies depend upon the educational system for the training and certification of its recruits. If the educational system were to increase its own fluidity, it could have a multiplied effect upon the social mobility of the whole society.

THE PROBLEMS OF PROFESSIONALISM

Another development in modern society that I would like to comment on briefly is the trend to organize everyone into professional categories. This is not confined to the formally licensed professions such as medicine or law, but is much more general. The modern craft union goes back historically to the old medieval guilds. Today we have organizations not only of plasterers, electricians, and doctors, but of morticians, real estate salesmen, air traffic controllers, university registrars, and so on. Everyone belongs to a guild or syndicate of one kind or another.

Some of these associations are very loose affairs whose programs are primarily social or educational, but many of them possess some form of regulatory power over the practice of the profession, and many more aim at achieving such power. Sometimes this power is exercised in order to protect the general public from quackery or fraud, but more often than not

29

its object is to protect the practitioners of the profession from competition. When an association announces that it is adopting a 'code of ethical practices' in order to 'raise professional standards,' you can usually be pretty sure that a drive is afoot to create a cosy little monopoly and to limit entry into the profession.

Many of these organizations have even achieved legal status for their regulatory powers – they act as arms of the state in policing the profession. And often we grant this power without even making sure that the regulatory activity will be carried out in a fair and non-discriminatory manner. The result is a weird tissue of ambiguities. We attack some restrictive and discriminatory practices with the law while at the same time we give to others its support and sanction. Professional and trade syndicates have been a potent force working against the social mobility of disadvantaged groups in our society, and I see no reason to believe that they will not continue to be so. This has been more of a problem in the United States because of the widespread discrimination against Negroes, but it has not been without significance in Canada, and it may continue to grow as such associations proliferate and acquire status and power.

I have singled out this problem for some special comment instead of treating it as an aspect of the social mobility question because of the special significance of the development of professional specialization in the field of knowledge. This is a fairly recent development – only about a hundred years old, I think. Before that time there were people who were biologists or chemists or physicians or economists, and they labelled themselves as such but not with the degree of exclusiveness in use today. If Joseph Priestley had called himself a chemist or

John Stuart Mill had called himself a Political Economist, this would have been more a prideful claim to the possession of a body of knowledge or a skill rather than an exclusive designation. Up to about the 1870s, most educated people were well read in all the various areas of human knowledge; to be a biologist, say, or a chemist, was merely to be especially well read in that field.

Today, by contrast, a professional designation in a particular field of scholarship or science is virtually a certificate of ignorance in all other fields. The academic scholar nowadays is the kind of person who can see a fly on a barn door at fifty feet but can't see the door, or even the barn. Most research work is carried out by ignoramuses of genius, who root out little truffles of empirical fact from the body of mother earth like a perigord pig on a leash, and who are about as equally concerned with the human significance of their work. There is the story (it may be apocryphal, but it could easily be true) of the scientist who was invited to attend a conference on 'the future of man' and declined the invitation on the ground that this was not his field!

I hate to give up any area of knowledge to the 'authorities' in the subject. It seems to me that there is an inherent medievalism in doing so; a danger of turning science into a kind of religion. It is especially dangerous to leave social science to the social scientists. There is very little in the social sciences that can be left exclusively to the economists and sociologists on the ground that it is purely technical. The welfare and the future of man are always involved, even in the most arid of our researches.

What disturbs me most, however, is not that professional

31

II:

Break
i
ng in upon modern trends of thought
has come the modern examination of the
media in which thought is expressed.
Understanding media becomes essential to
the mediation of our understanding.
Linear thinking gives way to the basic

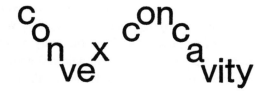

of multi-dimensional communication modes.
Lying within the reformation of science is
the counter-reformation of media psychology.

---

men in other fields do not discuss social questions, but that they so often do so with ignorance and prejudice, and the sublime assurance that usually accompanies them. Medical doctors will discourse on the economics of health services with less detachment than a drug salesman can muster. Professors of English literature will talk about the economy as if they could simply imagine it, like the plot of a play. Philosophers skilled in logical analysis will abandon everything they have been

Selectric media

ᴇxᴘLODE**S**

our consciousness, and

IMPLOᴅᴇs

society into a global village.

How else is it possible to understand the
thought and politics of those who are
too Jung to be Freudened into conformity?
In the media the meaning lies (and lies).
Therein is man's evolution: from the
:ll

electric technology of today's tomorrow,
through the Gutenberg revolution, right
to Piltdown Man.

---

taught, and have been teaching to others, in favour of assertions
about society beginning with 'It is obvious that ...' and followed
by some private piece of unsubstantiated, and often unsubstan-
tiatable, intuition. Some intellectuals have even rejected the
principle of scientific objectivity generally and totally, not only
in social questions, but for all fields of knowledge. Three ad-
miring students of Herbert Marcuse, for example, write that
'the essential element in Marcuse's teaching is that knowledge

33

is partisan' and that 'scientific objectivity, intellectual neutrality, and value-free thinking' are 'mere pretentions' which 'betray the goals of knowledge.' I tremble when I think of the other gods we are expected to worship instead. According to this view, Lysenko's practice of faking his genetics experiments in order that the results should agree with Stalin's political ideology would be the new wave of intellectual development.

I have probably gone far enough in this vein – you can plainly see that I am vexed, and I have probably bruised enough sensibilities already. I began by discussing the development of social science as a bright chapter in man's efforts to free himself from myth and tyranny, and I have now come around to saying that that great light has been dimmed by the development of intellectual professionalism which has led some of our best intellects to resign altogether from the discussion of social questions, and others to discuss them as simpletons and arrant drivellers.

Let us turn now to the problem of developing rational policy in a modern society.

THREE

Blueprints vs Little Steps

Someone once defined an economist as a man who is frequently in error, but never in doubt. There is enough truth in that to sting. A few years ago we used to play a little game of suggesting appropriate collective nouns for the various academic disciplines. We refer to a 'herd' of horses, a 'pride' of lions, and a 'flock' of geese; what should we call a group of chemists or historians or social scientists? The best of these terms that I can now recall was a 'fall-out' of physicists and a 'pretension' of economists. When one thinks of it, it really is pretentious to be a social scientist at all – to believe that one can make some sense out of the behaviour of that perverse, stubborn, opinionated, bigoted, and wilful creature, *homo sap.*; and even more pretentious to believe that some members of that species may find, and persuade others to be guided into, the paths of righteousness. In the course of the past century and a half, social scientists have suffered some heavy disappointments, but we are still plugging away, still believing that the world may be constructively changed by what we do. We are optimists, and that is perhaps the greatest pretension of all.

I noted earlier that the rise of social science in the nineteenth century was not viewed with enthusiasm by the established humane disciplines – literature and theology. The past hundred years or so has not stilled their criticism of our approach to the phenomenon of man, and we still find it expressed, sometimes sharply, today.

Some of these criticisms are merely puerile – like the recurrent theme of some humanists that social scientists talk nonsense because they often employ repellent technical language or jargon. During the past three years I have been on the board of editors of an academic journal whose interests lie primarily in literary interpretation, and I have had to read many manuscripts coming from the pens of literary scholars. I assure you that economists and sociologists have no monopoly of obscurantism or of professional jargon. The examination of the condition of man by means of the literary imagination is frequently opaque and badly written. Some other criticisms that I have seen of social science seem to be more profound than this, but they often call for one to try to understand man and to meet his problems on the basis of pure intuition rather than scientific knowledge, as a methodological principle. Even worse, they sometimes tend to enthrone ideology and doctrinal authoritarianism as the guides, or perhaps I should say the goads, of human action.

Nevertheless, as I have tried to point out, there are some insights of great value to be found in the humanist perception of man's nature, which social science has neglected. It may well be that the more we grow in economic wealth and the more we develop our society into one of industrialization, high technology, and urbanism, the more we should tune our ears

36

to what the humanists say about the state of our civilization.

I am returning to this now because I am going to discuss social policy, i.e. collective action to come to grips with our collective problems, and I want to emphasize the necessity of taking a large and comprehensive view of the objectives and effects of social policies. To say this, in such a general way, would seem to be merely to utter a platitude. But I think that there is little doubt that one of our major difficulties in doing what should be done in society is due to the fact that almost all of the policies initiated by governments are specific and *ad hoc*. They are directed at immediate and concrete economic or social or political problems and little or no attention is paid to their larger and cumulative consequences. Politicians and civil servants pride themselves on being 'practical men' and are impatient with people who raise issues which they regard as being 'philosophical' or 'academic.' My point is that, in the long run, it may prove to be very impractical not to be philosophical. The theme which will be the basis of what I have to say is that those who advise on, determine, and administer the policies of governments must be urged to adopt a much wider angle and a much longer focus of vision than they have customarily taken, if we are to deal adequately with the human problems of living in a modern society.

One of the things that I would like to do here is to try to make this view of the requirements of modern social policy concrete enough for use as a practical guiding principle. In order to do so, however, I will have to begin by discussing more generally the philosophy of social policy implied in this view.

The first point that I must make is a disclaimer. When I say that our social policies must be guided by more comprehensive and longer range goals, I do not mean that they must embrace the totality of life or that they must be cast into the framework of the grand sweep of history. At first sight it may seem as if such a disclaimer is unnecessary. Who is audacious enough to believe that he could prescribe, once and for all, the blueprint of the ideal society? But whether it is audacious or not, it has been one of the most common themes of social philosophy since Plato. You could fill a sizable bookcase with the writings of men who, over the course of western history, have dreamed of the perfect state and have committed their visions to paper. You could fill a whole library with the books that have been written as commentaries on these visions.

This is not a matter of interest only to people who dig around in libraries. During the nineteenth century dozens of communities were founded, most of them in the United States, by people who wished to turn their dream of social perfection into reality. Other dreamers, instead of going off into the American wilderness, set about to revolutionize their own societies and turn them into ideal states, and some of these dreamers succeeded, at least to the extent of creating the revolutions.

Moreover, this is clearly not a matter of only historical interest. The utopian cast of mind, if I may call it that, is an important feature of contemporary controversy in western social philosophy. The view that the particular evils of our society reflect a rottenness which is total; that reform of existing society and gradual progress are not possible; that one must start with a clean slate and build the new society without being constrained by existing institutions; that revolution is justified *in itself* because it 'cleans the slate'; the view that in order to build a just society one must create a 'totally new man': these are ideas which one will find expressed today on almost every college campus in the western world. Some people who hear them identify them as Marxist doctrine, and regard their exponents as simply a new wave of the 'communist conspiracy,' but in fact many of them are anti-Marxist and anti-communist. Marxism, after all, is not the only version of utopian romanticism in the history of political philosophy. When a person starts talking about how terrible contemporary society is and advocating its wholesale reconstruction, he may not be a Marxist or a communist; he may not even be a Christian!

He may not be a fool either, but the chances are that his prescription for social policy is very wrong and may be productive of much suffering and evil. During the Second World War, the philosopher Karl Popper wrote an important book called *The Open Society and Its Enemies*. The theme of the book is that the enemies of political freedom and social progress are those who have fallen under the 'Spell of Plato' and dream of creating a new society according to a specific blueprint. In their effort to wipe the slate clean of encumbering institutions, such people would cheerfully create misery and death on a wholesale scale. In their effort to create the new man, they would turn education into indoctrination. In their desire to carry the blueprint into realization, they would clamp an iron tyranny upon all people, and anyone who demurred would be shot as a 'counter-revolutionary.' When I first read Popper's book some fifteen years ago it seemed to me that he had presented an exaggerated picture. I no longer think so. I am reminded again of poor Urbain Grandier, who was fearfully tortured and burnt at the stake for the good of his soul by men who had the best interests of society at heart. We have to recognize that great evil can be done in the name of righteousness, that visionaries can be vicious, that a person who yearns for the millennium will welcome a cataclysm, and may not shrink from offering up human sacrifices.

Karl Popper's recommendation was that we avoid the evils of utopianism by adopting as our philosophy of social policy what he called 'piecemeal experimentation.' This view has been given further expression and development in recent years by the American political scientist Charles E. Lindblom who uses the term 'discrete incrementalism' to express the policy approach he advocates. The basic idea is that a society will best combine progress and freedom if its social policy consists of limited specific programs devoted to limited specific problems and undertaken by specific governmental agencies, without any effort to knit it all together in any comprehensive way. By this means, it is argued, we may experiment over a broad front by means of a great variety of policy efforts, and we can then follow through on those which are successful and abandon, without loss, those which are not.

I have great difficulty in accepting either of these two polar positions on the philosophy of social policy. I am willing to accept the view that the utopianism of comprehensive social planning would be a retrograde and possibly very dangerous philosophy, at least for a society such as ours which is already economically advanced, democratic, and socially progressive, and therefore has much to lose of great human value. It does not follow however that the only way in which we can preserve our achievements and make further advances is by confining social policies to narrow limits and short-range objectives. It seems to me that we can do better than that, and that we can do it safely. A social scientist, if he is realistic, will realize that to sit down to write the constitution of utopia is equivalent to nominating himself for dictator, or, if you like, 'philosopher-king.' But I don't think it is unrealistic for us to take the view that we can develop our specific social policies within an integrated framework of goals. The weakness of our economic and social policies at the present time is that they are in fact *too much* what Popper and Lindblom prescribe. They are too 'piecemeal' and 'disjointed,' and we could do better if we were prepared to be somewhat more comprehensive.

I would now like to give some brief illustrations which may help to make my argument here more tangible. My illustrations will be two areas of policy which have been of exceptional importance since World War II – housing policy and taxation policy.

Like most other countries, Canada has been engaged, over the past twenty years or so, in encouraging the construction of housing units by a variety of public policies. Housing policy has been, in the United States as well as in Canada, a clear case of the sort of thing that Popper and Lindblom have advocated: specific policies, strongly focused on specific problems and restricted to that focus. The problem of housing policy has been construed as the problem of building houses – it's as simple as that. Accordingly, policy in this area is merely a matter of making financial and other effective arrangements to draw the appropriate volume of the nation's productive resources into housing: the policy is measured and evaluated in terms of the number of units constructed.

The difficulty with such a policy approach is that when one builds houses, one is also engaged in the process of building a *city*. If we have a housing policy only and do not have a more comprehensive urban development policy into which housing fits, then it is unlikely that the city that will emerge will be the best possible city that civilized man can conceive and create. It may in fact turn out to be a very bad city indeed. Much of what has been written about the tawdriness of suburban living in North America is true; and much of the agonizing that has been going on over the decay of the central city is well founded.

A great many of our problems with respect to this aspect of modern life stem from a quite extraordinary gap between our image of man and the contemporary economic reality. We still think of man as labouring under the curse of Adam – expelled from the Garden of Eden and condemned to produce his bread by the sweat of his brow – and for most people that means being a farmer. Our literature and our philosophy alike have glorified the agriculturalist. Being 'close to the soil' and 'in communion with mother nature' are viewed as superior ways of life which carry with them virtue, goodness, and wisdom as necessary adjuncts. Some of you at least will remember a schoolroom in which you read Oliver Goldsmith's *Deserted Village* as an elegy for a bygone golden age of rurality, and the novels of Charles Dickens as warnings of the ineffable evil and misery inherent in city life. What is the widespread desire to own a detached suburban house on its own lot, with its own trees and garden, but a modern version of the family farm of earlier times? The ranch-style bungalow is a surrogate for a ranch.

One of the major problems of modern times is our inability to shake ourselves free of powerful rural images despite the fact that we are an urban and industrial people. Two members of this university, Professors Harvey Lithwick and Gilles Paquet, writing recently in their collection, *Urban Studies*, arrive at the conclusion that 'many of our present problems in both the urban and the regional environment stem from what may be called an agrarian or peasant view of economic reality. The changes brought about on the spatial organization of society as a result of economic development make this view archaic and irrelevant. Since it prevails in the hearts and minds of our policy-makers, it is little wonder that we have been notoriously unsuccessful in coping with both our urban and our regional problems.' That is, I think, a trenchant evaluation of the case. A colleague of mine at Indiana University, Professor Jerome Milliman, has pointed out that of the large expenditures made from the federal treasury in the United States for the purpose of social and scientific research, the U.S. Department of Agriculture had $262 million to spend last year, while the Department of Housing and Urban Development had less than $1 million: this in a country in which less than seven per cent of the population live on farms and which produces agricultural 'surpluses' that it finds difficult to get rid of. The situation in Canada is not appreciably different – the Department of Agriculture of the federal government is one of the largest anachronisms to be found in any modern state.

We have to come to grips with modern man as a city dweller in our social policies. The problem will be a real test of our ability to engage in comprehensive social planning and direction without falling into the error of constructing hard utopian blueprints. It is of more than passing interest that utopian philosophers have usually cast their visions of perfection in the form of ideal cities – from Plato's *Republic* to Ebenezer Howard's *Garden Cities of Tomorrow*. There is a danger of totalitarianism in the idea of city planning which it would be foolish for us to neglect, but we have to risk it. Great cities will not automatically come into being as a result of housing policy and urban transport policy, and city services policy and so on, all pursued in a piecemeal and disjointed way. We have to have urban policy. Modern man does not merely need housing, and buses and sewers. He needs a CITY in which to live.

I might add, before leaving this topic, that Canada is, at the present time, in a much more fortunate position than the United States. Canadian cities, it seems to me, are by and large promising – they have not yet met the needs of modern man, but they have not yet been ruined. Many American cities have become degenerate – so much so that some American social scientists have recommended that their centres be turned into parkland, with the focus of urban development shifted to the suburbs altogether. This, to my mind, is a council of despair and would amount to abandoning the opportunities of city life in the effort to solve some of its problems. The seriousness of the situation in the United States is indicated by the decision of the Nixon administration to create a cabinet-level Urban Affairs Council under the direct chairmanship of the President. It represents a major effort on the part of the national government to cope with the problems of city life. We will have to come to that in Canada too. I must add here that the urban problem in the United States intersects on so many planes with the racial issue that it is impossible to discuss the one without the other. Canadian cities have problems, but American cities are in a continuous state of explosiveness which reflects the racial crisis that now dominates American domestic life and thought. The new focus on urbanism which is emerging in American social policy is in large part a result of this intersection.

I now want to go on to discuss the other case that I have chosen to illustrate the argument put forward earlier: taxation. I have chosen this topic partly because of its importance as an instrument of public policy but also because it was the object of a royal commission investigation a few years ago which is of exceptional interest. The report of the 'Carter Commission' is a remarkable document in the history of public finance. But it is more than that – it is a landmark in the history of social policy.

What makes the Carter Report outstanding is its attempt to bring order into our system of taxation by providing the guidance of a set of general principles and general social goals. Traditionally, taxation has been used in the past as the string-pull for *ad hoc* economic and social policies of all kinds and descriptions. Whenever it has been decided to encourage one line of activity (like prospecting for uranium) or discourage another (like the consumption of alcohol) it is the power of the Royal Fisc that has been most often brought in to do the job. In this area we have been practising for many years the principles of social policy that Popper and Lindblom preach, and the result is absolute chaos. We now devote more highly trained talent to attempting to understand the tax laws, and to loophole them, than we do to administering them. Economists themselves have been an important factor in this accumulation of *ad hocery*. One of the things that economists feel fairly confident about is the economic analysis of the probable effects of taxes and subsidies, and since hardly anybody else seems to be able to talk sensibly about such matters at all, there has been a fairly clear field. But typically, economic advice on tax policy has been confined strictly to narrow specifics. I am quite sure that if, a few years ago, an economist in the Department of Finance or of Revenue had raised the issue of the general principles of taxation in relation to general social goals, the message would have come through to him loud and clear from on high: 'There is no future for you here – get thee to a university.'

But royal commissions are allowed to be philosophical about public affairs, if they choose to be, and the Carter Commission chose to be. I cannot here enter into a discussion of the Commission's proposals. It is sufficient to say that by adopting the view that equity in taxation demands that people should be taxed according to their incomes and that a person's income is measured by his acquisition of power to command the resources of the economy, the Commission laid the foundation for a coherent system of taxation. It could, in my opinion, have gone further than it did in elucidating the basic principles of social policy which taxation should serve; the commissioners could have been even more 'philosophical,' especially in defining the economic and social role of the modern business corporation and providing thereby better principles of corporate taxation, but this is a minor defect compared with the achievements.

I hardly need to mention that the public reception of the Carter Report has not been in accord with this interpretation of its merits. Most of the academic economists leapt to their feet and shouted 'bravo,' but almost everyone else hissed.

Some of the latter reaction is a bit hard to understand. It may have been nothing more than the simple ignorance of conservatism. (A French commentator on early nineteenth-century English politics once observed of Lord Liverpool, who was First Lord of the Treasury, that had he been present in Heaven on the first day of creation he would have exclaimed: 'Mon Dieu! Conservons le chaos!') I suspect, in addition, that peculiar vested interests accumulate around any complex and disjointed taxation system. After working the loopholes for many years, everyone becomes convinced that he is pretty good at it and that he picks pockets more deeply than he is picked from. The academic social scientist may believe that it is desirable to have a fiscal system that anyone can understand, but there are many taxpayers who think that it is in their interest to have one that no one can understand.

It seems very unlikely that the proposals of the Carter Commission will be directly implemented in Canada. Some academicians would count it failure if we did not set about the wholesale reconstruction of the system according to the Carter plan. If I have made my argument clear earlier, you will understand that I do not share this view. The role of general principles in social policy is not to present a blueprint for the construction of a wholly new structure. They are much more effective as guides for the gradual reconstruction of the old. We are not likely to tear down the old taxation system and erect a new one in its place and, if we did, we'd immediately set to work to make alterations in the new one.

We will always be making changes in our social policies, in taxation and in other areas. We need an architecture of social policy to guide not a master builder but the more pedestrian alterations carpenters who are constantly at work in a progressive society. The Carter Report will do its work if it acts as a general guide for the changes in taxation policy that will be made year-by-year in the future. Observers of tax policy and of public policy in general will observe Canada with great interest.

One of the reasons why the taxation system tends to become encumbered with all sorts of diverse (and sometimes incompatible) objectives instead of being used as a straightforward instrument by which to raise public revenues in a clear and equitable way, is because social policies in Canada have to be carried out within a political system of divided jurisdiction. The federal government can attempt to accomplish many things by fiscal policy which the constitution would constrain it from doing by other means. Federal states whose constitutions are old have had to be innovative in coping with the problems of the modern world, and most of the room available for exercising ingenuity in bypassing the restrictions of old constitutions has existed in the fiscal area of governmental power. I think that it is fair to say that Canada has been as ingenious as most federal states in coping with the problem. Yet, one cannot avoid the conclusion that one of the major barriers against the development of social policies appropriate to the modern world is the archaic form of the federal system. The federal system in Canada was enacted at a time when the nature of Canadian society was very different from what it is today. It may have been suitable when Canada was a nation of farmers, but it is not suitable for an urbanized industrial society.

In modern society, it seems to me that there are two levels of government that are meaningful, the nation and the city. The nation corresponds, in a broad way, to the political self-consciousness of a people; it is an area within which there is a free flow of goods and services and of their factors of production; it represents, in most cases, a satisfactory scope for the development of economic and social policies; and, in a world composed of nation-states, a national government has an important role to play in controlling the country's relations (both friendly and hostile) with other sovereign powers. The city is important because it is the actual environmental entity in which most people live and work. By contrast, the province (and the individual state in the United States) is, in the modern world, an anachronism. It does not correspond to anything that can provide an effective scope for social and economic policy. I am all in favour of a high degree of governmental pluralism, but I cannot see what merit there is in carving up the country almost arbitrarily into large geographical segments and giving those segments quasi-sovereign political powers. Political divisions of this sort can only be troublesome for a nation that ought to develop coherent social policies – and they may even actively frustrate the functioning of some policies of great importance. (If a province, for example, in an effort to attract persons of wealth and influence, offers them the incentive of low or zero inheritance taxation, it will work powerfully against the achievement of greater economic equality and social mobility which should be one of the modern state's primary aims.)

It is for this reason that I do not think that one should dismiss out of hand the suggestion of some of the French-Canadian separatists that Canada should be reconfederated into two almost sovereign nation-states. Some of the suggestions that have been made are clearly retrograde, and would be a threat to economic development and social progress, but the idea of separatism is not inherently bad. When the British North American provinces united into a confederation in 1867, those who conceived the constitution had in mind the need to avoid the chief weakness that had manifested itself in the American federation – the excessive power of the individual states. But the events did not unfold according to this scenario. For a variety of reasons, many of which could not have been foreseen, governmental power became decentralized in Canada while the opposite trend was taking place in the United States. Today, Canada is a weak federation and the United States a strong one.

Now I do not want to be misunderstood on this point. I am not saying that French-English separatism is the *only* way of achieving a framework of governmental organization that can be adequate to the demands of modern social and economic policy. It is possible that within the framework of the existing constitution Canada as a single nation could regroup its governmental powers in a satisfactory way. What I *am* suggesting is that separatism might be another way of doing this – more radical, perhaps more dangerous, but not by any means impossible or entirely undesirable. In any case, if a modern industrial society is to meet the social challenges which such a society generates, it must accomplish somehow a form of governmental organization which permits the formulation and effective implementation of social policies at two fundamental levels – that of the nation, and that of the city or metropolis. Power, finance, and political and bureaucratic talent must flow towards these two poles of social development, and the political entities which are, socially and economically speaking, *non*-entities, i.e., the provinces, correspondingly reduced in importance.

I have become increasingly more specific, but I have, I think, come to the end of what I can fruitfully do here in that direction, and I want to return now to more general topics.

FOUR

The Essence of Liberalism

A large part of my time as an academician during the past twenty years has been spent in the study of the history of economic and social thought. One of the viewpoints which people who work in this field are likely, after a little while, to adopt, is that there is nothing new beneath the sun. We have neat labels for particular viewpoints or sets of ideas and it is fairly easy for us to stick one or more of them onto any contemporary argument and thereby identify it, just as a biologist would identify an insect. We have a fairly large selection of labels to choose from, such as liberalism, capitalism, socialism, communism, conservatism, individualism, pluralism, anarchism, utilitarianism, romanticism, fascism, and so on.

The trouble, though, is that the common, and even the academic, meanings of these labels do not stay constant. Anyone who has studied the political and economic thought of the past two centuries must be aware of the great changes that have taken place in political terminology. Many important words have acquired new connotations and some have changed their meanings almost completely. George Orwell wrote about this in his novel *Animal Farm*, suggesting that perversion of language may be employed as an instrument of political tyranny, and there is no doubt that he was on to something. But the terms we use in political discourse can also go through great shifts of meaning, even the 180° ones that Orwell satirized, as a result of an evolutionary process. The deliberate perversion of political language for nefarious purposes is undoubtedly an important feature of the Age of Propaganda in which we live, and it has made rational and informed discussion of social questions more difficult. In contemporary political discussion words are regarded as invested with ideological content and many of them are viewed by some as 'codes' for disguised or unconscious political ideas. In some circles, for example 'order' is a bad word and 'protest' is a good one, while in others it is the other way round. Some people seem to believe that one makes a coherent political argument by shouting or displaying in print a single word like FUCK or SHIT, and perhaps they are right if they get an emotional and irrational reaction from others by doing so. Personally, I feel rather deprived by this development; it mean that one cannot employ profanity for art or emphasis without risking a political identification. For a Nova Scotian like me that represents a definite decline in the standard of living. It may be that, in time, these extremities of speech will enlarge and enrich the language, but in the meantime we find ourselves almost incapable of rational political discourse because of the wholesale destruction of objective terminology.

Nevertheless, we must keep on talking about political and social problems. To fall silent in the face of intellectual bullying is no different from being silenced by the censor or the political police.

This is by way of edging around to the terminology that I find it necessary to employ in order to indicate what is, in my view, an appropriate philosophy of social policy for the modern world. I have struggled with the problem during the past few years and have had to discard some old and favourite pieces of intellectual lumber. The central pillars remaining are 'rationalism' and 'liberalism.'

I am aware, of course, that there are some quarters where these terms, especially 'liberalism' are a stench in the nostrils. In some contemporary discussion in the United States 'liberalism' denotes only the vileness and hypocrisy of those in established positions in the society – some people use it as if *it* were a strong, rich, four-letter word. And this is not confined to the practitioners of 'guerilla theatre' in the streets, but has extended itself into intellectual discussion. A short while ago I wrote an article on John Kenneth Galbraith in an academic journal which circulates almost exclusively to economists. Among my 'fan mail' arrived a postcard from New York saying, 'Good for you – that article on Galbraith. He has been the *Lolly Pop* for all Lazy Parasitical Middle Class Sweet Liberals. He is the Rasputin of the Liberal Escapists.' I reread my article quickly to see what could have caused such a remarkable outburst. I can only conclude that my correspondent was already loaded, and that I had simply touched his hair-trigger somehow. There seems to be quite a bit of political emotion primed and ready in our society at the present time, and if I had Jeremy Bentham's ability to invent new words altogether, or Marshall McLuhan's talent for obscurity, I would be tempted to talk about modern social problems in one, or both, of those styles. But that wouldn't really help.

55

'Liberalism' is a difficult term to use in expressing a modern social philosophy, not only because it makes some people see red (in two different senses for two very different opponents of it) but because it is one of those terms that have gone through the evolutionary process of alteration in meaning that I mentioned earlier.

The early nineteenth-century philosophy of liberalism was highly individualist. Society was conceived of as fundamentally a collection of individual persons, and individual freedom to pursue one's own interests was regarded as a principle which not only had a sound philosophical foundation, but would work more effectively than any other to promote the practical objectives of economic progress. The early nineteenth century liberals were not doctrinaire laissez-fairists – they did not advocate that there should be *no* state interference in the economy – but they did view the role of the state as small and, generally, they were sceptical of the idea that the state as an institution could be an instrument for the effective promotion of human and social objectives.

It was the liberals themselves who undermined this position – by working so effectively to increase the democratic representativeness of the state and to improve its administrative capacity. By the latter part of the nineteenth century, the term 'liberalism' was adopting other connotations and resonances – it was being invested with the ideas of equality of opportunity, economic security, humaneness, amelioration, generosity – and the state was being invoked as an institution which should take upon itself the duty of promoting these social objectives. From being a philosophy that looked upon the coercive power of the state as an evil, always to be deplored, though sometimes necessary, liberalism became, in the English-speaking world at least, the leading philosophy of the positive, active, interventionist state which uses its power for the purpose of promoting a wide range of desirable social ends. This shift has been so complete that, today, the set of political ideas which used to be called 'liberalism' are now most commonly called 'conservatism.' (In the game of political philosophy it is hard to identify the players without a historical score-card.) Some modern writers on political philosophy reject this political infidelity of our language and wish to restore the older meaning of the term 'liberalism' as a conveyance for the idea of strict individual freedom and responsibility, but they only succeed in confusing the discussion of important matters by attempting to exercise a proprietary interest in words.

The essential theme of liberalism, both old and new, it seems to me, is that the only valid purpose of society is to serve the welfare of the individuals of which it is composed. Only individuals are valuing entities. Societies, races, nations, etc., even families, are collectivities; they are not sentient organisms and it is invalid to ascribe to them qualities of sense and sensibility which apply only to individual beings.

Considered in these terms, it is plain that nothing fundamental hinges upon any abstract conception of the proper role of the state in modern life. The state is merely instrumental. It is not the embodiment of the 'national soul'; it does not represent the 'genius of the race.' Phrases such as these (and there are lots of them) are meaningless. There is, as a consequence of this view, no merit as such in having a large or small scope for state action; it all depends on what will best serve the welfare of the nation's citizens considered as individuals. At the present stage in modern society, we need the services of a large and active state, because there is much that we wish to accomplish that cannot be done otherwise. The liberal philosophy is essentially one of grappling with the affairs of the world in a rational and pragmatic way, without the constraints of dogma. But even more so it is the realization that the political work of man will never be finished. He must go on and on. The road may be marked as leading to Utopia, but one of its essential features is that it never gets there.

A great deal of what is fundamental in the political philosophy of liberalism was well expressed by Sir Wilfrid Laurier many years ago. Of all the writers on this subject, I find that he remains fresh and relevant, and I want to quote him to you.

The principle of Liberalism is inherent in the very essence of our nature, to that desire for happiness with which we are all born into the world, which pursues us throughout life and which is never completely satisfied. ... We constantly gravitate towards an ideal which we never attain. We only reach the goal we have proposed ourselves, to discover new horizons opening up, which we had not before even suspected. We rush on towards them and those horizons, explored in turn, reveal to us others which lead us even further and further ...

This condition of our nature is precisely what makes the greatness of man, for it condemns him irrevocably to movement, to progress ... There is always room for improvement of our condition, for the perfecting of our nature, and for the attainment by a larger number of an easier life.

Then he went on to sound a warning:

Experience has established that invariably, imperceptibly, abuses will creep into the body social and end by seriously obstructing its upward march, if not endangering its existence. ... There will always be men found, who will attach themselves with love to these abuses, defend them to the bitter end and view with dismay any attempt to suppress them. Woe to such men if they do not know how to yield and adopt proposed reforms! They will draw upon their country disturbances all the more terrible that justice shall have been long refused ... Wherever there is repression, there will be explosion, violence and ruin. I do not say this to excuse revolutions, as I hate revolutions and detest all attempts to win the triumph of opinions by violence. But I am less inclined to cast the responsibility on those who make them than on those who provoke them by their blind obstinacy.

This passage is from a speech of Laurier's to the Canadian Club of Quebec in 1877. He had just become leader of the Liberal party and he felt it necessary to say to his French Canadian compatriots that liberalism was not a religious heresy; that a Catholic is more likely to suffer damnation on earth if he opposes social change than he is to do so in the after-life by embracing it. It was a frankly partisan speech, and Laurier did not distinguish between the Liberal party and liberalism as a political philosophy, but that does not diminish the wisdom or the modern relevance of his reasoning.

It is clear from what I have been saying on my own account, and from the passage I have quoted from Wilfrid Laurier that reform and change are essential to the liberal philosophy. But make no mistake about it. This is no effort to preserve the *status quo* by giving small concessions that will hush the demand for far reaching and fundamental social change. The history of the past two centuries gives eloquent testimony to the fact that it is the liberal rationalists not the revolutionary romantics, who have been the true radicals. While most of the rest of the world has been engaged in the fruitless process of exchanging one tyranny for another, the countries that have adopted a liberal political philosophy have moved long distances along the road to a civilized and humane society, and they have also kept open the opportunity for continued progress in this direction. That is no cause for complacency. We are not civilized enough by any means. Our society is still very far from being generous and just. Liberalism still has a great deal of work to do.

I cannot, at this point, embark upon the description of a detailed agenda for liberal action in the modern world. If I were to do so, I would take up again the four large 'problems' outlined above, and I would lay the greatest emphasis upon the need to prevent our society from hardening into entrenched oligarchies of wealth and power. Especially, I would talk long and loud and strongly about the obligation that falls upon the educational system to widen the opportunities for advancement and to increase the fluidity of our society.

I am not unaware of the difficulties, both philosophical and practical, that one encounters in translating the philosophy of liberal rationalism into social policy, and indeed, I have scattered a few of the larger ones here and there in these lectures. I return to the theme with which I began: the social sciences have a special role to play in making a political philosophy of this sort coherent and practical. They are committed, it seems to me, to a liberal point of view, and they are an essential part of our long struggle to bring reason and truth to the study and discussion of social questions.

Man is a perverse being – full of superstitions, and grand and petty passions, and assorted bigotries – but he is also endowed with the capacity to reason, and he can be gentle and generous upon occasion. We have had some very dark periods during the past two centuries since the modern economic and social world began to come into being, but liberality and rationality have survived and, on the whole I think, have expanded and deepened their capacity. It is the *special* task of the social scientist to carry them further, but it is an obligation that does not belong to him alone. To bring the spirit of science to the discussion of human affairs, to dispel the mists of dogma and mysticism in the study of social questions, is a prime responsibility of all men of learning.

I cannot honestly say that we can be proud of the way in which intellectuals, especially those of academia, have been meeting these responsibilities in recent years. I do not wish now to enter into a recital of our failings but there are times when I think that our entire commitment to the search for truth is in grave danger. Some large part of that danger, it seems to me, is due to our pursuit of narrow professionalisms, our implicit rejection of the wider responsibilities of scholarship. I have been thinking lately of the legend of Dr. Faustus and reflecting upon the fact that Faustus was a professor – a

man of learning, a scientist, a good research man. As you recall, he sold his soul to the devil. But none of the artists who
have written the great statements of the legend tell us plainly
what it is that Faustus got in exchange. That may be the reason
why the story continues to have such great evocative power:
the soul of an intellectual can be sold and paid for in many
currencies – wealth, power, fame, popularity, fashion, youth,
certainty – all these will serve. In most versions of the story,
Dr. Faustus is saved from hell at the eleventh hour by the love
of a pure maiden. Well, salvation is not quite as easy as that,
and even if it were, there probably aren't enough pure maidens
to go round. Altogether it is an implausible ending to a great
dramatic statement. But that is not what seems to me to be the
legend's greatest weakness. As I read it, the story implies that
if the intellectual goes to hell he goes alone, and the other good
people remain behind to mourn his personal folly. That is a
profound error. If the intellectual goes to hell, he carries
civilization down with him.

Now this may be a good place for me to end – because I
have come back to my beginning. When I started these lectures,
the gates of hell were opened wide and I discussed the demonic
possession of the nuns of the Carmelite Convent at Loudun
and the great witchcraft scare and other assorted intellectual
frenzies of the sixteenth and seventeenth centuries. And then
those gates closed with the arrival of the eighteenth-century
enlightenment and the dawn of the Age of Reason. Now it
seems as if I see them opening again and you will be wondering
whether the poor Plaunt lecturer of 1969 is obsessed with
thoughts of the devil and may undergo a religious conversion
before your very eyes. Have no fear. I do indeed hear the

62

hinges creaking sometimes and it seems to get pretty hot in Academia upon occasion. But the only bolts and bars that can suppress man's barbarity are reason of mind and liberality of spirit. Whatever the attacks made upon us, and from whatever quarter, those are our proper weapons, and, with them, we shall overcome.